IRAQ

Paul Mason

mc **Marshall Cavendish**
Benchmark
New York

(handwritten: J 956.7 Mason)

Marshall Cavendish Benchmark
99 White Plains Road
Tarrytown, NY 10591
www.marshallcavendish.us

First published in 2008 by
MACMILLAN EDUCATION AUSTRALIA PTY LTD
15–19 Claremont Street, South Yarra 3141

Visit our website at www.macmillan.com.au or go directly to www.macmillanlibrary.com.au

Associated companies and representatives throughout the world.

Mason, Paul, 1967-
    Iraq / by Paul Mason.
    p. cm. –(Global hotspots)
    Includes index.
    ISBN 978-0-7614-3180-0
    1.Iraq–Juvenile literature.I. Title.
    DS70.62.M37 2008
    956.7–dc22

                                                        2008018685

Produced for Macmillan Education Australia by
MONKEY PUZZLE MEDIA LTD
The Rectory, Eyke, Woodbridge, Suffolk IP12 2QW, UK

Edited by Daniel Rogers
Text and cover design by Tom Morris and James Winrow
Page layout by Tom Morris
Photo research by Lynda Lines
Maps by Martin Darlison, Encompass Graphics

Printed in the United States

Acknowledgments
The author and the publisher are grateful to the following for permission to reproduce copyright material:

Front cover photograph: People flee the burning town of Basra in March 2003 following the invasion of Iraq by US and
British forces. Courtesy of Getty Images (Mirrorpix).

Corbis, pp. **4** (Faleh Kheiber/Reuters), **6** (Bettmann), **11** (Slahaldeen Rasheed/Reuters), **15** (Bettmann), **17** (Bettmann), **18**
(Sygma), **20** (Michel Setboun), **24** (UNSCOM/Sygma), **26** (epa), **29** (Faleh Kheiber/Reuters); Getty Images, pp. **7** (AFP), **8** (AFP),
9, **10** (AFP), **13** (Hulton Archive), **21** (Roger Viollet), **22** (Time & Life Pictures), **23** (AFP), **25** (AFP), **27**, **28**; iStockphoto, p. **30**;
Rex Features, p. **19** (Sipa Press); Topfoto, p. **16**.

While every care has been taken to trace and acknowledge copyright, the publisher tenders their apologies for any
accidental infringement where copyright has proved untraceable. Where the attempt has been unsuccessful, the
publisher welcomes information that would redress the situation.

1 3 5 6 4 2

CONTENTS

Glossary words

When a word is printed in **bold**, you can look
up its meaning in the Glossary on page 31.

ALWAYS IN THE NEWS

Global hot spots are places that are always in the news. They are places where there has been conflict between different groups of people for a long time. Sometimes the conflicts have lasted for hundreds of years.

Why Do Hot Spots Happen?

There are four main reasons why hot spots happen:

1 Disputes over land, and who has the right to live on it.

2 Disagreements over religion and **culture**, where different peoples find it impossible to live happily side-by-side.

3 Arguments over how the government should be organized.

4 Conflict over resources, such as oil, gold, or diamonds.

Sometimes these disagreements spill over into violence–and into the headlines.

HOT SPOT BRIEFING

IRAQ'S PEOPLES
Most of Iraq's people are Arabs. Their ancestors were **nomads** who lived in the **Middle East** thousands of years ago. In the north are the **Kurds**, whose territory stretches into Iran and Turkey as well.

The aftermath of a car bomb explosion in Baghdad, Iraq. Explosions such as this mean Iraq is constantly in the news.

Iraq

Iraq has been a global hot spot since 1980. Then, its leader Saddam Hussein launched a war against neighboring Iran. Ever since, Iraqis have regularly been in conflict with either their neighbors or one another.

Iraq is part of an ancient land, one of the birthplaces of modern civilization. How did it become a global hot spot? The answer lies in Iraq's mixture of peoples, and its turbulent history.

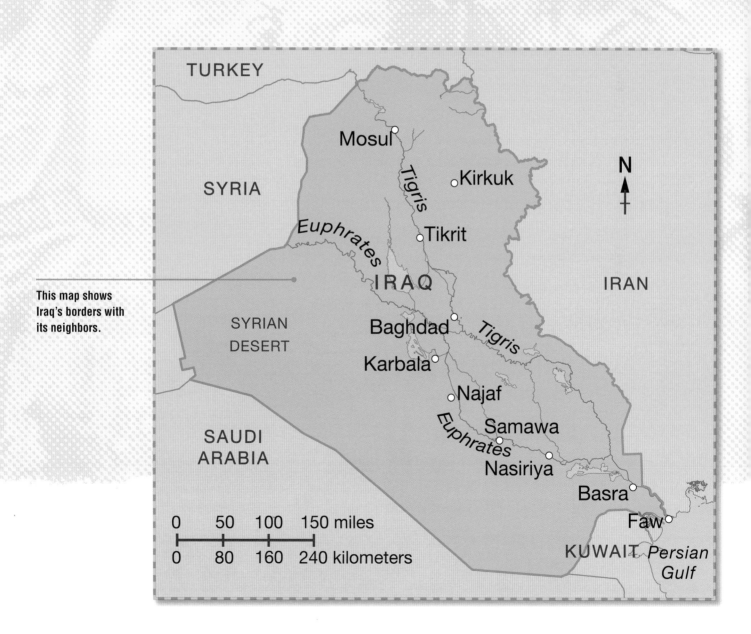

This map shows Iraq's borders with its neighbors.

TURKEY

SYRIA

Mosul

Tigris

Kirkuk

Euphrates

Tikrit

IRAQ

IRAN

SYRIAN DESERT

Baghdad

Tigris

Karbala

Najaf

SAUDI ARABIA

Euphrates

Samawa

Nasiriya

Basra

Faw

KUWAIT Persian Gulf

N

```
0     50    100   150 miles
|—————|—————|—————|
0     80    160   240 kilometers
```

BIRTHPLACE OF CIVILIZATION

The modern country of Iraq lies in an ancient land called Mesopotamia. More than 5,000 years ago, Mesopotamia was one of the places where human civilization began.

The Culture of Mesopotamia

The ancient Mesopotamian culture was based in the river valleys of the Tigris and Euphrates. These valleys were home to the world's first **irrigation** systems. Irrigation meant that farmers had extra crops to sell, so that other people no longer needed to grow their own food. This allowed the first cities to grow up here.

The Hanging Gardens of Babylon, one of the Seven Wonders of the Ancient World, were near the modern city of Baghdad, Iraq.

"If we fear bad luck when we see a black cat, or count time in twelve hours for each day and night, or look up to the stars to read our fortune … it was the civilization of ancient Iraq which invented these things."

Leonard Wooley, archeologist.

The Landscape

The landscape of Mesopotamia, and modern Iraq, is varied. At its heart lie the Tigris and Euphrates Rivers. Outside these **fertile** areas, most of the land is dry and harsh. In the northeast, there are tall mountains near Iraq's border with Iran and Turkey. This region is also home to rich oilfields, areas where oil is found under the ground. In the southwest and west, most of the land is desert.

People have gone fishing in the Tigris River for more than 7,000 years.

Different Rulers

In 539 BCE, Mesopotamia became part of the Persian Empire. For the next 1,000 years and more, Mesopotamia was controlled by rulers who came from outside the region:

- In 331 BCE Persia was conquered by the Greek leader Alexander the Great, who also took control of Mesopotamia. Within 200 years, though, the Persians had retaken power.

- In 637 CE, Arab invaders defeated the Persian rulers of Mesopotamia and took control.

RELIGION

In 637 CE, Muslim invaders from Arabia took control of the land we now know as Iraq. They brought with them the religion of Islam. This new religion soon became a cause of conflict, as it still is today.

The tomb of Ali.

Divisions in Islam

In 656 CE, worshippers of the religion of Islam began to have bitter arguments. The argument was about who should be leader:

- On one side was Ali, the cousin and son-in-law of the founder of Islam. Ali was supported by a *shi'a*, which means **faction**. His supporters became known as Shi'ite Muslims.

- On the other side were religious chiefs who chose a different leader. Their supporters were known as Sunni Muslims.

Eventually, most Muslims became Sunni. Only in Iraq, and neighboring Iran, were the Sunnis outnumbered by Shi'ites.

HOT SPOT BRIEFING

DEATH OF ALI
The Shi'ite Muslim leader Ali was murdered in Iraq in 661 CE. Today, Ali's shrine is the third-holiest site in the world for Shi'ite Muslims.

Iraq and Iran

Religious links between Iraq and Iran are one reason why Iraq is a global hot spot today. Iran is a Shi'ite country, run according to Islamic ideas. Since 1979, the United States and many of its **allies** have seen Iran as an enemy. Iraq's population is about 60 percent Shi'ite Muslim, so the United States has feared that Iran and Iraq might act together to become very powerful in the Middle East. This has led the United States and other countries to support governments in Iraq that were opposed to Iran.

HOT SPOT BRIEFING

IRAQ'S OTHER RELIGIONS
About 5 percent of Iraq's people belong to other religions. Most of these non-Muslims are Christians.

Today, religion is a major cause of conflict in Iraq. This Shi'ite Muslim mosque was blown up by Sunni Muslims.

DIFFERENT CULTURES, ONE COUNTRY

Most people living in Iraq today are Muslim Arabs, but there are people from other **ethnic** backgrounds living there as well. Divisions between the different groups are a cause of conflict in Iraq today.

The Kurds

Kurdish people are the largest non-Arabic cultural group in Iraq. The Kurds are different from their neighbors. They have different homes, cooking, and clothes, and different attitudes to women. Their homeland, Kurdistan, stretches across the mountains where the borders of Iraq, Iran, Syria, and Turkey meet. Kurdistan has never been a country, but many Kurds have always wished it were. After World War I, the Kurds thought that they would get their own country, but instead their territory became part of these other nations.

Men working in the fields of Iraqi Kurdistan. Kurdistan is a mountainous area divided between Iraq, Iran, Syria, and Turkey.

HOT SPOT BRIEFING

RELIGION IN KURDISTAN
Like most Iraqis, nearly all Kurds follow the Muslim religion. However, they are mostly Sunni Muslims, unlike the majority of Iraqis, who are Shi'ites.

Iraqi Kurdistan

As well as being a large homeland spread between countries, Kurdistan is the name of a smaller area in northern Iraq. After World War I this area came under the control of the Iraqi government. The Kurds who live there had always wanted to be independent and they resented Iraqi control.

"Some villagers came to our chopper. They had fifteen or sixteen beautiful children, begging us to take them to hospital. So ... we were each handed a child to carry. As we took off ... my little girl ... died in my arms."

A photographer describes a gas attack on the Kurdish town of Halabja in 1988. Most observers blame Iraq for the attack.

A Kurdish woman sits with a picture of her children. They died during the gas attack in 1988.

ARAB NATIONALISM

Arab nationalism is the idea that Arab peoples, whose ancestors came from the Arabian Peninsula, should be united under one leadership, in a country of their own. This idea first became popular in the early 1900s, and became important in Iraq during the 1950s.

Living Under the Ottoman Empire

At the time when Arab nationalism first appeared, most Arabs were living in regions controlled by the Ottoman empire. Although it had once been very powerful, the Empire had lost a lot of its territory and influence. Czar Nicolas I of Russia called it "the sick man of Europe." This encouraged the Arab nationalists to think that they might be able to split away from the Ottoman Empire.

HOT SPOT BRIEFING

THE OTTOMAN EMPIRE
During the 1500s and 1600s, the Ottoman Empire was the most powerful in the world. It controlled areas in the Middle East, including Iraq, Europe, Asia, and Africa.

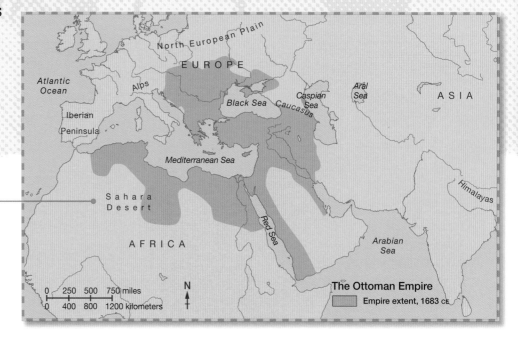

This map shows the area governed by Ottoman rulers when their empire was at its largest.

World War I

In 1914, World War I broke out. The Ottoman Empire sided with Germany and its allies. On the other side were Britain, France, and their allies. The British encouraged the Arabs to fight the Ottomans. They hoped that Ottoman troops would be kept busy fighting the Arabs, and would not be able to join the fighting in Europe.

Arab Hopes

The Arabs hoped that if the Ottoman Empire was defeated, they would be able to have their own country. However, this was not to be. The British and French had secretly agreed to carve up the Arab lands between them.

HOT SPOT BRIEFING

NATIONALIST POLITICS
The two main Arab nationalist groups are Nasserites and Ba'athists. They agree on these key points:
- they are anti-Western and anti-Israel
- they both support Arab unity and modernization.

Arab fighters in the desert during World War I, preparing to attack Ottoman troops.

THE KINGDOM OF IRAQ

The Kingdom of Iraq was formed out of areas of the old Ottoman Empire that were controlled by Britain. This is why Iraq today has so many different religions and cultures living inside its borders.

Carving Up the Middle East

At the end of World War I in 1918, Britain and France divided up the old Ottoman territories in the Middle East between them. Britain took control of what would become Iraq, Israel and Palestine, and Jordan. At the time, it was not clear how these territories would be divided. Some Arab nationalists hoped that they would not be divided at all. But the British took little notice of what local people wanted.

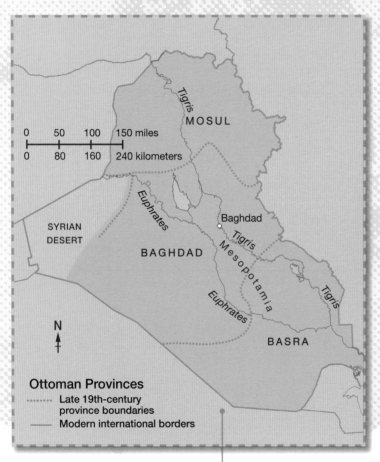

Ottoman Provinces

- - - - - Late 19th-century province boundaries
───── Modern international borders

Modern Iraq, with the old Ottoman provinces from which it was formed.

HOT SPOT BRIEFING

THE DISCOVERY OF OIL
During the 1920s and 1930s, large reserves of oil began to be discovered in Iraq. The largest oilfields are in the northern Kurdish areas and in the south, near the border with Kuwait.

The Formation of Iraq

The British decided to form several new countries from parts of the old Ottoman territory. Iraq was one of these new countries, formed mainly of the old Ottoman provinces of Mosul, Baghdad, and Basra. The British thought that Iraq should have a king, someone that all its different peoples could look up to. They chose Faisal I. Faisal had led the Arab revolt against the Ottomans during World War I but he was almost unknown in Iraq.

"There is still no Iraqi people, only masses ... connected by no common tie, prone to anarchy [lawlessness], and always ready to rise up against any government."

King Faisal I of Iraq.

King Faisal I (center) with his brothers and advisors. Faisal was not from Iraq. His family came from Mecca, Saudi Arabia.

MILITARY RULE AND THE BA'ATH PARTY

Iraq became independent in 1932, but strong ties with Britain remained. The British wanted to keep their influence in this oil-rich country, but it was eventually ended by a revolution in 1958.

The Monarchy Is Overthrown

In 1958, the **monarchy** in Iraq was overthrown by a **military coup**, led by General Qassem. King Faisal I, the prime minister, and other leading politicians were murdered. The new government, led by Qassem, was Arab nationalist. It stopped British oil exploration and set up the Iraqi National Oil Company. It took land from rich farmers and gave it to the poor.

General Qassem waves to the crowds after forcing his way to power in 1958.

"Iraq's treaty with Britain was forced on the Iraqi people."

Saddam Hussein, future ruler of Iraq, speaking in 1972 about the treaty that had allowed Britain to influence Iraqi politics after World War I.

Politics by Force

Qassem's coup in 1958 set a pattern for new governments to take power by force rather than through **democratic elections**. Qassem himself was overthrown by a group of army officers in 1963.

Military Coup, 1968

In 1968, a third military coup changed the government in Iraq. This coup was led by another general, named Bakr. General Bakr's coup bought the Ba'ath Party to power. The Ba'ath ruled Iraq for almost forty years, until 2003, when Ba'ath rule was ended by the United States-led invasion.

HOT SPOT BRIEFING

NATIONALIZATION

Nationalization occurs when a country decides that industries should be owned by the country, rather than by individual companies. Soon after coming to power, General Bakr started to nationalize the oil industry. He wanted the profits from oil to go to the government, rather than making company owners rich.

In 1973, an international shortage of oil caused a worldwide oil crisis. Prices skyrocketed, making countries such as Iraq much more wealthy.

SORRY... out of gasoline WILL REOPEN MONDAY

SADDAM HUSSEIN

In the mid-1970s, President Bakr became increasingly unwell. Bakr's place was gradually taken by his right-hand man, Saddam Hussein.

Saddam Hussein the Enforcer

Saddam Hussein's main job for Bakr had been to enforce the Ba'ath Party's grip on power. Those who opposed them ended up in prison, or were put to death. Hussein is said to have killed many of his opponents himself. As he became more powerful, Hussein began to bring his family members and people from his home town of Tikrit into the government.

Saddam Hussein (front) in 1979 as the new president of Iraq, with some of his soldiers.

Saddam Hussein Becomes President

Saddam Hussein became president of Iraq when Bakr resigned in 1979. He continued to use brutality and violence against anyone who opposed him. When he came to power, Hussein killed a quarter of Iraq's governing council, as well as hundreds of other people he thought might challenge him.

Increasing Military Strength

As soon as Saddam Hussein became president, he began to make Iraq's army stronger. Hussein bought weapons from the United States, Russia, and elsewhere. His scientists began to research **chemical and biological weapons**, such as poison gases. Iraq also bought the nuclear fuel uranium, leading other countries to fear that Hussein was trying to develop nuclear weapons.

A military parade in the Iraqi capital city, Baghdad, 1990.

"Keep your eyes on your enemies, and be faster than them. Don't provoke a snake unless you have the intention and power to cut off its head."

Saddam Hussein explains key leadership ideas in his book, *Great Lessons, Commandments to Strugglers, the Patient and Holy Warriors* (2002).

WAR WITH IRAN

In 1979 a revolution in Iran brought Shi'ite Muslims to power there. They decided to govern Iran according to Islamic law. Saddam Hussein was worried that this could encourage Shi'ites in Iraq to challenge his authority.

Saddam Hussein Attacks Iran

Apart from his concern about the Shi'ites in Iraq, Saddam Hussein had several other reasons to think that attacking Iran might be a good idea. He:

- thought that after the revolution, Iran might not be ready to defend itself very well
- wanted to grab the oil-rich areas just over the border, where many people spoke Arabic
- wanted to control the whole length of the Shatt el-Arab waterway leading from the Iraqi city of Basra to the Persian Gulf.

On September 2, 1980, Iraqi troops attacked Iran.

Foreign Support for Saddam Hussein

Other Arab countries supported the war on Iran. One of these was Kuwait, which lent Saddam Hussein $14 billion. The leaders of many of these countries did not like the idea of being overthrown by their people in the same way as the former leader of Iran. They hoped Hussein would crush the Iranian revolutionaries. Some Western countries also supported Hussein, with money, weapons and **intelligence** information.

Iranian leader Ayatollah Khomeni arrives in Iran after the revolution in 1979.

Outcomes of the War

Iraq's war with Iran finally ended in August 1988, and it had been a disaster for Iraq. Saddam Hussein had not achieved any of his aims. The war left Iraq with enormous debts. The oil industry had been damaged, and Iraq's economy was almost ruined. Iraq had once been a wealthy country, but now it was a poor one.

UNBALANCED FORCES

Iraq had more of just about every kind of weapon than Iran throughout the Iran–Iraq war.

WEAPON AND DATE	IRAQ	IRAN
Tanks, 1980	2,700	1,740
Tanks, 1987	4,500	1,000
Fighter planes, 1980	332	445
Fighter planes, 1987	500 +	65
Helicopters, 1980	40	500
Helicopters, 1987	150	60
Artillery, 1980	1,000	1,000 +
Artillery, 1987	4,000 +	1,000 +

Iraqi troops at a river crossing near the border with Iran in 1980. The tank in the background was probably paid for with loans from other countries, which Iraq would later struggle to pay back.

ATTACK ON KUWAIT

Since 1961, Iraq's leaders had been claiming that neighboring Kuwait should really be part of Iraq. In 1990, Saddam Hussein launched an invasion of Kuwait, aiming to make it part of his territory.

Reasons for the Invasion

Saddam Hussein's main reason for invading Kuwait was money. After the Iran–Iraq war, Iraq owed Kuwait vast sums. Making Kuwait part of Iraq would wipe out the debts. Income from Kuwaiti oilfields would help repair the damage caused by the Iran–Iraq war.

HOT SPOT BRIEFING

IRAQ'S CLAIM
Saddam Hussein claimed that Kuwait had once been part of the Ottoman province of Basra from which Iraq was partly formed. He said that it should have become part of Iraq in 1921, along with the rest of Basra.

The Invasion Succeeds

The invasion of Kuwait was a success for the Iraqi forces. The Kuwaiti ruling family fled to Saudi Arabia, and there was almost no **armed resistance**. Iraq soon had control of the whole of Kuwait.

Iraqi forces occupy Kuwait City in August 1990.

The World Reacts

Around the world, almost all leaders condemned Saddam Hussein's invasion of Kuwait. When the Iran-Iraq war ended, the **United Nations** (UN) had assembled an international **coalition** to drive the Iraqi forces out of Kuwait. In February 1991, the coalition forces attacked, and within days the Iraqis had been defeated. Roughly 100,000 Iraqis died in the fighting.

Aftermath of War

When the war ended, the United States and Britain established "no-fly zones" over northern and southern Iraq. Iraqi aircraft were not allowed in these areas. The Kurds in the north could no longer be attacked by Iraqi fighter planes or helicopters. It became impossible for Saddam Hussein's forces to control the area, and the Kurds began to govern themselves.

Left-behind wreckage, abandoned by the Iraqi army as it fled along the road from Kuwait back to Iraq.

"I will not allow this little dictator to control 25 percent of the world's oil."

President George H. W. Bush speaking about Saddam Hussein after Iraq had invaded Kuwait in 1990.

WEAPONS OF MASS DESTRUCTION

After his defeat in the invasion of Kuwait in 1991, Saddam Hussein continued to be in conflict with the United Nations. The biggest problem concerned Hussein's Weapons of Mass Destruction, or WMDs.

Conditions of Peace

After the Iraqi defeat in Kuwait, the United Nations set conditions on Iraq's future behavior. It said Iraq had to:

- pay compensation to Kuwait and others harmed in the invasion

- give up its WMDs, which were mainly chemical and biological weapons that it had been developing for years, including the missiles that could be fired hundreds of miles into other countries.

Until these conditions were met, Iraq was not allowed to trade with other countries. The flow of profits from the oil industry became a trickle. As a result, life became increasingly difficult for ordinary Iraqis.

Destruction of banned Iraqi weapons after the 1991 war.

Weapons Inspections

The United Nations suspected that Iraq still had some WMDs hidden away. Between 1991 and 2003 the UN sent teams of "weapons inspectors" to try and find them. Some weapons were destroyed straight after the war, but later on the inspectors could not find any WMDs. They were unsure whether this was because Iraqi officials were being unhelpful, or because there were no weapons left to find.

An Iraqi soldier watches as UN weapons inspectors leave their headquarters to search for WMDs in December 1998.

SEPTEMBER 11, 2001

STATISTICS

On September 11, 2001, Islamic **terrorists** crashed hijacked airplanes into U.S. targets. At the World Trade Center in New York, 2,750 people died, and 24 are still listed as missing. In an attack on the Pentagon, 184 people died. Another 40 people died when United Airlines Flight 93 was crashed by **terrorists**. In response President George W. Bush made a speech accusing three countries of being part of an "Axis of Evil" that had to be stopped. They were North Korea, Iran, and Iraq.

INVASION

In 2003, U.S. President George W. Bush declared that the threat posed by possible Weapons of Mass Destruction in Iraq was too great. He and his advisors decided that Saddam Hussein had to be removed from power.

Support for the Invasion

President Bush struggled to get support for attacking Iraq. Most other countries thought that the UN weapons inspectors should be given more time to look for Iraq's WMD. Only the British, Australian, and Polish governments would agree to send troops to help the invasion. Even so, the United States went ahead.

The Invasion Begins

On March 20, 2003, the invasion of Iraq by U.S. and British forces began. They were supported by small numbers of troops from Australia, Denmark, and Poland. In all five countries there were bitter objections to the war, which their governments ignored.

"We are ready to sacrifice our souls, our children, and our families so as not to give up Iraq. We say this so no one will think that America is capable of breaking the will of the Iraqis with its weapons."

Saddam Hussein before the U.S.-led invasion of Iraq in 2003.

Saddam Hussein, shortly after being captured hiding in a hole in the ground in December 2003.

Defeat for Saddam Hussein

The strength of the U.S. military and their allies meant that Saddam Hussein's forces were quickly defeated. By April 9, 2003, Baghdad, the **capital city**, had been captured and Hussein had fled.

HOT SPOT BRIEFING

LOOTING THE NATIONAL MUSEUM
The Iraqi National Museum in Baghdad held some of the world's oldest **archaeological** treasures. In the days following the invasion, **looters** broke into the museum and stole many of these.

Chaos Reigns

Chaos followed the invasion. Policing and government fell apart, and the invading soldiers could not keep order. The old rivalries between different religious and cultural groups sprang up again. Shootings, kidnappings, and bomb attacks became common, and life for ordinary people got worse and worse. No WMDs, which had been the reason for the invasion, were ever found.

Looters stole or destroyed many treasures in the National Museum in Baghdad.

A CHALLENGING FUTURE

Iraq faces a challenging future. The removal of Saddam Hussein did not bring Iraq stability and peace. Instead, Kurds, Shia, and Sunni all began to compete for power and resources.

Establishing Order

The U.S.-led forces found it impossible to restore law and order after Saddam Hussein's defeat. The police and the army were full of Hussein's supporters from the Ba'ath Party, and it was felt that they could not be trusted. This meant that there was no one able to stop crime, and so murder, bombing, and torture became everyday risks for many ordinary Iraqis.

Ruined Infrastructure

Iraq's infrastructure (its water and power supply, and transportation system) was in ruins. It would remain in ruins for a long time. By the middle of 2008, even people living in Baghdad still could not rely on electricity or clean water for their homes.

"From the invasion until now we have seen nothing from the government. Every day they say they are going to provide electricity, but they do nothing."
Jinan Obaidi, Baghdad resident, 2007.

Iraqis queue for petrol. Since the invasion, many goods have become hard to get in Iraq. Even petrol, which Iraq has plenty of, can be impossible to buy.

Hope for the Future

There is some hope that Iraq may have a peaceful future. In Anbar Province, where Sunni resistance to the invasion first started, the violence has slowed down. In Baghdad, the violence has also eased, and people feel safer walking on the streets.

Most of all, Iraq now has a democratic government, which was elected in January 2005. As the government takes more power back from the invading forces, Iraqis of different backgrounds have the chance to work together for a better future.

DEATHS IN THE CONFLICT

As the conflict in Iraq continues, the death toll continues to rise:
- By November 2007, more than 4,000 of the invading troops had been killed
- Estimates of the number of Iraqi civilians killed vary widely. The lowest estimate is 74,000. The highest is more than a million.

Iraqis celebrate after voting in 2005 to elect the country's first democratic government for almost fifty years.

GEOGRAPHY

Capital Baghdad

Area 168,000 square miles
(437,072 square kilometers)

Main rivers Tigris and Euphrates

Climate Cool winters in the south, freezing in the north. Hot summers, especially in the south

Land use Farmland 14%

Uncultivated (mainly desert) 86%

PEOPLE

Population 27,499,638

Rate of population change +2.6% per year

Life expectancy 69.3 years

Average age 20 years

Religions Muslim 97%

(Shi'ite 60–65%, Sunni 32–37%)

Christian and other 3%

Ethnic groups Arabs 75–80%

Kurds 15–20%

Other 5%

Literacy Men 72%

Women 51%

THE ECONOMY

Agricultural products Wheat, barley, rice, vegetables, dates, cotton, cattle, sheep, poultry

Industries Petroleum, chemicals, textiles, construction materials, food processing, fertilizer, metal processing

Main exports Crude oil, food, animals

Gross Domestic Product per person* $3,600

National earning by sector Agriculture 5%

Industry 68%**

Services 27%

(**mainly oil)

* Gross Domestic Product is the total value of all the goods and services produced by a country in a year divided by the number of people in the country.
(Source for statistics: *CIA World Factbook*, 2008)

The flag of Iraq

GLOSSARY

allies supporters

archeological to do with archeology, which is the study of ancient cultures through the things they left behind

armed resistance opposition from soldiers or ordinary people using weapons

capital city city where the government of a region or country is based

chemical and biological weapons chemical weapons are deadly chemicals, such as poisonous gases, and biological weapons spread deadly diseases

coalition temporary alliance between one or more groups

culture things that make a group of people distinctive, such as their language, clothes, food, music, songs, and stories

democratic elections opportunity for every qualified person to vote on who the government should be and how the country should be run

ethnic describing a group of people who have similar culture and, sometimes, physical appearance

faction smaller group within a larger one, and which disagrees with the larger one about some of their beliefs

fertile able to grow living things well, such as food crops

intelligence secret information, gathered without an opponent or enemy knowing

irrigation adding water to soil to make it better able to grow crops

Kurds mountain-living people whose territory lies on the borders of Turkey, Syria, Iraq, and Iran

looters people who use the aftermath of a disaster to steal items

Marsh Arabs Shi'ite Muslim people who live in the southern areas of Iraq

Middle East region stretching from northeast Africa to southwestern Asia and southeastern Europe, usually said to include Bahrain, Cyprus, Egypt, Iran, Iraq, Israel, Jordan, Kuwait, Lebanon, Oman, Qatar, Saudi Arabia, Sudan, Syria, Turkey, United Arab Emirates, and Yemen

military coup change of government forced by the military, usually led by army officers and backed up by armed force

modernization starting to use the latest available ideas, techniques, and equipment

monarchy system of government that has a king or queen at its head

nomads herders who move from place to place to find food for their animals

terrorist person or people using violence to scare others

United Nations organization set up after World War II that aims to help countries end disputes without fighting

INDEX

DISCARD